W9-COJ-727

DATE DUE

President Lyndon Baines Johnson

Cornerstones of Freedom

The Story of
THE
GREAT SOCIETY

By Leila M. Foster

 CHILDRENS PRESS®
CHICAGO

Lyndon B. Johnson (left) with John F. Kennedy

Library of Congress Cataloging-in-Publication Data

Foster, Leila Merrell.

   The story of the Great Society / by Leila M. Foster.
     p.   cm. — (Cornerstones of freedom)
   Summary: Describes the social reform work done by
President Johnson and the significant legislative
accomplishments through which he hoped to help blacks and
the poor of America.
   ISBN 0-516-04755-8
   1.   United States—Politics and government—1963-
1969—Juvenile literature. 2.   Johnson, Lyndon B.
(Lyndon Baines), 1908-1973—Juvenile
literature. [1.   United States—Politics and
government—1963-1969. 2.   Johnson, Lyndon B.
(Lyndon Baines), 1908-1973.] I. Title. II. Series.
E846.F65   1991
973.823—dc20   90-22445
                                    CIP
                                     AC

PHOTO CREDITS

AP/Wide World Photos—Cover, 1, 2, 4, 5, 6 (2 photos),
8 (left), 11, 14, 15, 18, 20 (2 photos), 22, 23 (3 photos),
24 (left), 25, 26, 27, 31
UPI/Bettmann Newsphotos—7, 8 (right), 9, 10 (2
photos), 12, 16, 17, 19 (2 photos), 21 (2 photos), 24
(right), 28, 29 (2 photos), 30, 32
(Cover—President Johnson campaigning in front of
portrait of the late President Kennedy)

Page 2: President Johnson making a radio-TV
broadcast to the American people

"President John Kennedy is dead." From Dallas, Texas, the news flashed round the world on November 22, 1963, bringing shock, grief, and questions. Who was the assassin? What would the new president do?

The new president was Lyndon Baines Johnson. He had been chosen as vice president in the Kennedy administration to balance the ticket of the Democratic Party. Johnson was an older Texan politician while Kennedy was a youthful contender from Massachusetts. Kennedy had won the election of 1960 by a narrow margin, defeating then-Vice President Richard Nixon, the Republican candidate.

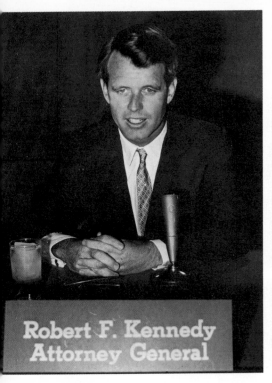

Robert F. Kennedy
Attorney General

The first task facing the new president was the need to assure the country and the world of a smooth transition of power. On the advice of Attorney General Robert Kennedy, Johnson was sworn in as president of the United States on *Air Force One* before it took off from Dallas. The Secret Service people protecting the president were anxious to get Johnson back to the safety of the White House because of the fear that there might be a conspiracy to kill other members of the government.

The new president wanted to accomplish many things during his administration. On the night he was sworn in as president, Johnson outlined for his associates his hopes for new legislation in the fields

6

of education, civil rights, and medical care.

Five days after taking office, Johnson spoke to a joint session of Congress and promised to continue the plans of the Kennedy administration. Indeed, Johnson's Great Society program followed in the footsteps of Franklin Delano Roosevelt's New Deal, Harry Truman's Fair Deal, and John Kennedy's New Frontier. However, Johnson's Great Society program went much further. The federal government became involved in many aspects of the social and economic life of Americans.

Johnson's years of political experience and the country's need to regroup after Kennedy's assassination worked in his favor. Also, a lull in the Cold War gave the new president a chance to focus on domestic policy.

President Johnson meeting with Whitney Young, executive secretary of the National Urban League

What Was the Great Society?

Johnson described the Great Society program in his book, *The Vantage Point: Perspectives of the Presidency 1963-1969:*

> The Great Society was described with different words at different times. In substance, I saw it as a program of action to clear up an agenda of social reform almost as old as this century and to begin the urgent work of preparing the agenda for tomorrow. The program we submitted to the voters during the 1964 campaign would commit the nation to press on with the War on Poverty, to provide greater educational opportunities for all American children, to offer medical care to the elderly, to conserve our water and air and natural resources, and to tackle the country's long-standing housing shortage.

Sioux Indian children in South Dakota (left) participate in a Head Start program. Mrs. Lyndon B. Johnson reads to children (right) in a Washington, D.C., Head Start program.

Johnson saw his Great Society program as a realistic plan that the United States could achieve in a reasonable period of time, and not as an impractical ideal.

Eventually, his ideas were translated into legislation for voting and other civil rights, health and school aid, programs like Head Start (classes for needy preschoolers and their parents), VISTA (Volunteers in Service to America—a domestic Peace Corps), financial aid to economically depressed Appalachia, and community action programs throughout America.

The Great Society was committed to quality integrated education for all children.

Federal examiners signing up African-American voters in Canton, Mississippi, as provided by the Voting Rights Act of 1965.

But even people who agreed that these were desirable goals had questions about whether the federal government should run such programs. Why should federal authorities get into areas where state governments or private charitable groups were already active? Could the government—and the taxpayers—afford to pay for all these projects? And would the federal government simply grow larger and less efficient if it took on these tasks? Would bureaucracy stifle creativity in handling such issues?

Opponents to the new legislation argued that citizens would be weakened in the long run with this kind of government handout. And the government would be forced ever deeper into debt to pay for all these projects.

President Johnson ignored these critics. He was a master politician who used his personality to dominate the Washington scene. Johnson made himself the central focus of his administration. In his book, Johnson said: "I was President of the United States at a crucial point in its history, and if a President does not lead he is abandoning the prime and indispensable obligation of the Presidency."

President Johnson shaking hands with admirers on a campaign tour of the South in 1964

Civil rights leaders meeting at the White House during the Kennedy administration (left to right): Martin Luther King, Jr.; Attorney General Robert Kennedy; Roy Wilkins; Vice President Johnson.

Leadership, however, requires the ability to build a general agreement. For Johnson, general agreement meant deciding what needed to be done and then convincing Congress and the American people to do it.

Also, having served in Congress as the majority leader, Johnson knew how to influence legislators. He knew what they wanted—recognition for their work. And he knew what they feared—loss of influence. So Johnson encouraged Congress to participate in planning some of the Great Society projects, while keeping his other ideas private so that opposition could not develop.

Through meetings and briefings with members of Congress, Johnson involved himself in the traditionally legislative function of enacting bills. He encouraged his staff to consult with congressional leaders and find out how his friends and enemies would vote for specific projects. Johnson's sense of timing regarding when to send bills to Congress, his judgment on which leaders should introduce the legislation, and his choice of committees to involve in the passage of the bills were all brilliant, and instrumental in achieving his goals.

For example, John Kennedy was unable to get a bill passed to authorize federal aid to education. The bill failed because of the opposing views of two major lobbying groups—the National Education Association, representing the public schools, and the National Catholic Welfare Conference, representing parochial schools. Johnson, however, would not let his education bill go to Congress until he had worked out a compromise with these two groups. In Johnson's bill, the money would be given—not to the schools—but to the children who needed aid. Then the president sent his bill to Congress—and he had his Elementary and Secondary Education Act within four months.

Johnson compared Congress to a dangerous animal. If you are trying to train such an animal, you have to know how much to push it before it turns on you. You need to know the animal's moods each day and time your actions accordingly.

Johnson's performance with the American people in the 1964 election was also impressive. Running against Republican candidate Senator Barry Goldwater, Johnson was perceived as the one who wanted peace in Vietnam, while Goldwater was seen as a man who wanted to increase United States

Barry Goldwater addresses a crowd in Marietta, Ohio.

involvement in Vietnam. Johnson's Great Society program promised voters a brighter future. Johnson was seen as a man who helped people. It was a landslide victory for Johnson. He had captured 61 percent of the votes cast.

Civil Rights Legislation

Three days before he left the presidency, Johnson was asked what he considered his "greatest accomplishment." He replied that it was the response of Congress to his Voting Rights Act. That civil rights act made it possible for African-Americans to rise to positions of leadership by removing some of the barriers that kept blacks from voting.

Three major pieces of civil rights legislation were passed during the Johnson administration:

Civil Rights Act of 1964—Prohibits discrimination in public places and helps ensure fair employment and desegregated schools

Voting Rights Act of 1965—Eliminates literacy tests and poll taxes as a condition for voting

Civil Rights Act of 1968—Outlaws discrimination in the sale or rental of housing and interference with voting, work, schooling, jury duty, or participation in federally assisted programs.

Many Americans consider this civil rights record a remarkable achievement.

African-Americans voting in the Mississippi Democratic primary election

From the day he took office, Johnson fought to get Congress to pass the civil rights legislation that Kennedy had proposed. The bill guaranteed equal access to public accommodations and equal employment opportunity. Most of the bill's supporters expected that, at best, a modified version might make it through the congressional committees. However, Johnson sent a clear message through public and private channels that he would not compromise on this issue—the bill would be voted either up or down as it stood.

The fate of the bill rested on whether or not its supporters could get a vote of *cloture* (a parliamentary procedure to set time limits on debate), thereby

In 1966, African-Americans voted in large numbers for the first time in history. This polling place is in Alabama.

removing the threat of a *filibuster* (talking a bill to death by blocking other legislation). Republicans under the leadership of minority leader Senator Everett Dirksen joined with liberal Democrats led by Senator Hubert Humphrey. A two-thirds vote of the 100 senators voting was needed to pass the motion of cloture. The final vote was 71 to 29—just four more votes than was necessary. Although other changes were proposed, the victory had been sealed and those proposals were voted down. The bill, signed into law by Johnson on July 2, 1964, was the most sweeping civil rights legislation of the twentieth century up to that time.

Senators Everett Dirksen (left), Hubert Humphrey (center), and Herman Talmadge (right) worked for the Civil Rights Act.

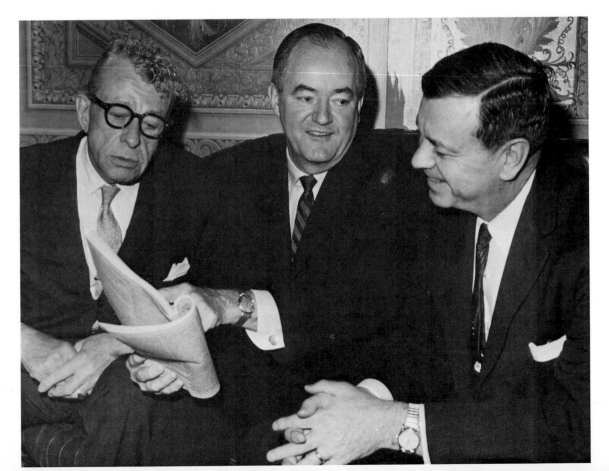

Martin Luther King, Jr. (left), holds up a picture of three civil rights workers murdered in Mississippi in 1964. Four African-Americans died in the bombing of their church in Birmingham, Alabama (right), in 1963.

Tension was great that summer. Three civil rights workers were murdered in Mississippi. Churches in the South were bombed because of their support for civil rights. In the North, riots broke out in New York and in four other cities. A long hot summer of violence brought calls for law and order.

After his landslide 1964 election, Johnson called on Attorney General Nicholas Katzenbach to begin drafting another civil rights bill dealing with equal voting rights. The president discussed the legislation early in 1965 with several black leaders, including Roy Wilkins of the National Association for the Advancement of Colored People (NAACP) and Martin Luther King, Jr., of the Southern Christian Leadership Conference (SCLC), Whitney Young, Jr., of the National Urban League, Clarence Mitchell of the NAACP, A. Philip Randolph, and others. Although the chances of passing this bill did not look bright, it was decided that Johnson would support it in government and the black leaders would take it to the people.

Part of the latter campaign was the 54-mile

Left: President Johnson talks with civil rights leaders (left to right): Roy Wilkins; James Farmer; Martin Luther King, Jr.; and Whitney Young. Right: Clarence Mitchell, Jr., head of the Washington Bureau of the NAACP

Civil rights marchers (left) in Selma, Alabama, were turned back at this bridge. A "Spirit of '65" fife and flag corps (right) leads off a civil rights march in Montgomery, Alabama.

march of blacks and whites to Selma, Alabama, on March 7, 1965. When state troopers injured more than 50 of the marchers, Johnson was criticized for not sending in the federal troops immediately. But his sense of timing had told him that any such action would have pushed moderate Southerners into the opposing camp. So, instead, President Johnson waited until Governor George Wallace requested federal aid—the state of Alabama was unable to bear the financial burden of mobilizing the National Guard and could not otherwise protect the marchers. Johnson then signed an executive order federalizing the Alabama National Guard.

On March 15,
1965,
President
Johnson told a
joint session of
Congress that
the time had
come to
guarantee
every
American the
right to vote.

After consulting with the Democratic and Republican leadership, the president decided to address a joint session of Congress on the subject, to show bipartisan support and to let the people see that action was being taken to deal with the civil rights issues. Referring to the efforts of African-Americans to gain equality, he said:

> Their cause must be our cause too. Because it is not just Negroes, but really it is all of us who must overcome the crippling legacy of bigotry and injustice. And . . . we . . . shall . . . overcome.

The president received a standing ovation. More important, his speech helped bring about the passage of the legislation. Four months later, Johnson signed the bill into law.

Not all the civil rights legislation sailed through Congress so quickly, however. Shortly after the Voting Rights Act of 1965 was signed, the Watts riots erupted in Los Angeles. The effort to pass fair-housing legislation was blocked by a month-long filibuster in 1966 and by committee action in 1967.

Johnson decided not to give up on the fair-housing issue, as some advised, but he did not try to impose the provisions of the bill by executive order because

Looting and burning during the 1965 riots in the Watts section of Los Angeles

Left: The mule-drawn wagon carries the casket of Martin Luther King, Jr., in a procession on the streets of Atlanta. Right: A trooper stands guard over a devastated neighborhood during the Washington, D.C., riots of 1968.

of the strong public sentiment against them. Congressional action seemed the only possible way to deal with discrimination in housing. The Senate passed the bill on March 11, but House approval was by no means sure.

Then on April 4, 1968, Martin Luther King, Jr., was assassinated. His death touched off riots in Washington, D.C., and 125 other cities around the country. In this crisis situation, the House approved the omnibus Civil Rights Act of 1968, which included provisions prohibiting discrimination in the sale and rental of housing. The bill also made it a federal crime to interfere with voting, work, schooling, jury duty, or participation in federally assisted programs. Penalties for rioting were increased.

Justice Thurgood Marshall, appointed by Johnson and the first black justice on the United States Supreme Court, congratulated Johnson on his civil rights achievements: "Thank you, Mr. President. You didn't wait. You took the bull by the horns. You didn't wait for the times. You made them!"

If the Great Society was so great, why didn't Johnson run for another term as president? Clearly, Johnson had many other things he wanted to do. He said that he left Washington feeling "so little have we done, so much have we yet to do."

President Johnson announcing the appointment of Thurgood Marshall (right) as Supreme Court Justice

Johnson also realized that every president lost or used up political support as his term wore on. That was one of the reasons he pushed so hard for his legislative programs after his landslide 1964 election. In addition, the division of public opinion about the Vietnam War and his failure to bring about peace there had resulted in diminishing popularity for Johnson.

His health was also a factor. The president had suffered a heart attack in 1955 and had been hospitalized twice for surgery while he was in the White House. With a family history of heart problems, he feared the possibility of disability while he was in office.

President Johnson working on the speech in which he announced that he would not run for reelection

And the country's condition was not good. Taxes had to be raised to support the war effort and pay for the Great Society programs. Raising taxes would have been out of the question if Johnson were also to run again for president.

Also, the likelihood of more riots in the summer of 1968 was strong. As president, Johnson might be required to send in federal troops again—not a good prospect for a presidential candidate.

Besides, Johnson believed he could help to defuse the war issue by coupling his announcement not to run with his decision to focus on a peace effort in Vietnam and halt the bombing.

So on March 31, 1968, Johnson announced that he

On March 31, 1968, President Johhnson told the nation that he would not seek or accept the nomination of his party for another term as president.

27

Chief Justice
Earl Warren
(left)
administers
the oath of
office to
President
Richard M.
Nixon.

would not run. Hubert Humphrey became the Democratic candidate. Humphrey lost the election to Richard Nixon.

In retrospect, how was the Great Society viewed? Senate Democratic leader Mike Mansfield reportedly said: "We have come too far too fast during your administration. The people want a little let-up and a little rest." Others quipped that the slogan of the Great Society was "We shall overdo."

While blacks and the poor might benefit from the Great Society, the majority—especially the middle class—were not happy with all the social changes

The "Southern Caravan" (left) of the Poor People's March treks through the South on the way to a rally in Washington, D.C., in 1968. Supporters of gun control (right) in Cleveland, Ohio, speak with presidential candidate Hubert Humphrey.

being forced on them. Even among those who might benefit most from the changes, there was dissatisfaction—the laws had not brought the changes they expected.

And objections were raised to the increased power of the executive branch of government and to the federal takeover of state and local affairs.

Economic problems were created by the entrance of the federal government into so many new areas. The programs were not properly funded, resulting in a devalued dollar, an increasing national debt, and growing inflation.

Demonstrators
in Albany, N.Y.,
protest
Governor
Rockefeller's
proposed cuts
in welfare
spending

The more the government moved into new programs, the less freedom individuals had to make their own decisions.

Along with the federal dollars came bureaucratic control, and paperwork that swamped businesses and educational institutions.

When Johnson was leaving office, he told Senator Barry Goldwater that the Great Society programs were not working but he didn't know why. Although money and effort were being poured into these programs, there were limits to what the government could do for its citizens.

Johnson has been praised for his good intentions and attempts to help the needy, even by people who did not agree with his programs. The civil rights acts are probably his greatest contribution to shaping a different society from the one he faced when he took office. The amount of legislation that he was able to get passed was phenomenal and testified to his political abilities in dealing with Congress. Unfortunately, many of his accomplishments on the domestic front were overshadowed by growing hostility toward the Vietnam War.

Johnson died on January 22, 1973. Just the day before, President Nixon, who had won a second term, announced a cease-fire in Vietnam and plans that ended many of the Great Society programs.

Funeral of President Lyndon B. Johnson (1908-1973) in Washington, D.C.

President Johnson greets young Head Start graduates in 1965.

INDEX

About the Author

Leila Merrell Foster is a lawyer, United Methodist minister, and clinical psychologist with degrees from Northwestern University and Garrett Evangelical Theological Seminary. She is the author of books and articles on a variety of subjects.